SCARS

**WRITTEN AND ILLUSTRATED BY
PARENT/CHILD TEAM OF
DAVE, JULIAN, AND NOELLE FRANCO**

DEDICATIONS:

This book is dedicated to the fighting men and women who make our neighborhoods and all the fun and terrifying, life-changes, experiences, and friendships possible.
—The Franco Family

To my loving husband, "magical" Noelle, and "precious" Anna: I believe in you.
—Lynn Dubenko, Ph.D.

I dedicate this book to the wonderful students and families at Sage Canyon Elementary.
—Janet Orr

To Quinn and Teagan, my heros.
—Dr. Adria O'Donnell

To my wife, Annie, who helps me remember that I belong.
—Stew Montgomery

To my supportive husband and 3 beautiful daughters who support me with my dream to help children to climb over "their rocky mountain" and discover a rainbow of hope on the other side.
—Colleen C. Ster

CHARITY:
Wounded Warriors Foundation

SALES:
The student author and illustrator of this book will be distributing a portion of their earnings into their college savings funds.

4114U: How to Read and Use this Book

Dear Reader,

You may be reading this story for pleasure, or you may have chosen this book because you can relate to its subject matter. Either way, here are some helpful instructions to navigate and guide your way through this book:

1. Read and enjoy the story and notice the vocabulary footnotes; remember the story was written by a parent/child team and illustrated by kids just like you. If you have experienced peer pressure or some other life-changing event, ask yourself if the characters in this story feel the same emotions you have experienced.

2. After you read the story, you will find a section called 4114U. This section has been put together by experts to give you some helpful tips and advice on how to work through your peer pressure situation, as well as other significant events in your life. You will find activities to do by yourself along with some helpful activities to do with a parent or loved one.

Because true healing requires you to focus on your emotional, educational, social, and even spiritual needs, we have divided the 4114U portion of the book into the following three sections:

- Action Steps to Help Families Emotionally
- Action Steps to Help Families Socially
- Action Steps to Help Families Spiritually

One of our goals is for you to feel like this book was written just for you; we want you to see that many other people struggle with life-altering events just like the one you are experiencing. We also want to give you some hope that things will get better, and to empower you (and your parents) by providing the necessary tools needed to deal with peer pressure.

While we hope you will find this book helpful, please keep in mind that its content is not intended to be a substitute for any professional medical advice, diagnosis, or treatment. We hope you enjoy this book.

All the best,

Colleen C. Ster

President/Publisher, Reflections Publishing

Acknowledgements

A wise elementary principal once told me that our job as parents and educators is to teach our children the coping tools they need, so when they find themselves in a difficult situation, like experiencing peer pressure or getting bullied, they will have the appropriate tools to access. This is the mission of Reflections Publishing—to allow children to help their peers through the power of their stories and illustrations, and to allow experts to equip kids with the tools needed to thrive in today's world.

This book would not have been possible without the numerous brainstorming and editing sessions with the following people. I thank you for your many hours of dedication and passion to this mission.

Colleen C. Ster
President/Publisher of Reflections Publishing

Educators: Peg Conrad, Kim Hogelucht, Jan Menconi, Janet Orr, Kim Mowry, and Erica Rood

Business Professionals: Heather Davis, Beth Misak, Jen Tankersley

Child Psychologists/Family Therapists: Melissa Bolt, MSW; Karen Clark-San Diego Rescue Mission, FT trainee; Lynn Dubenko, Ph.D; Richard Griswold, Ph.D - School Psychologist AF/SC; Adria O'Donnell, Psy.D; Lewis Ribner, Ph.D; Linda Sorkin, MA, LMFT

Student Editorial Team: Hans Hogelucht, Garrett Ritchie, Alexandra Ster, Caroline Ster, Isabelle Ster, and Megan Tankersley

Table of Contents

Chapter 1: Eyes Closed, Tie Undone	1
Chapter 2: A Terrific Place for a War	5
Chapter 3: Wanna Play with Sumpthin'?	10
Chapter 4: The Gang	29
Chapter 5: Mark and the Muscle	40
Chapter 6: A Change of Plans	50
Chapter 7: Good Luck	64

4114U Section

Introduction	72
Action Steps to Help Families Emotionally	73
• Peer Pressure Cycle	73
• Tug of War: Mental Battle	74
Action Steps to Help Families Socially	76
• Self Reflection Checklist	77
• Parent/Kid: Friendship Checklist	78
• Kids: Ways to Make New Friends	79
• Who's in your Friendship Bucket? Activity	80
• Kids: Fitting in With Peers	82
• Parents: Understanding the Peer Pressure Cycle	83
• Parent & Kids: Role Playing Scripts/Write your Own	84
Action Steps to Help Families Spiritually	86
About our Experts	88
Reference Section	90
In-Depth 4114U Concepts	93
Book Club Discussion Questions	94

Published by Reflections Publishing
© 2011 Reflections Publishing.

All rights reserved. No part of this book may be used or reproduced in any manner whatsoever without the prior written permission of the publisher, except for brief quotations embodied in critical articles and reviews.

This book is a work of fiction. Names, characters, businesses, organizations, places, events, and incidents either are the product of the author's imagination or are used fictitiously. Any resemblance to actual persons, living or dead, events, or locales is entirely coincidental.

First Edition. Published in the United States of America.

ISBN 978-1-61660-003-7

Visit our website at www.reflectionspublishing.com for more information or inquiries.

* * *

Other books by Reflections Publishing:

The Real Beauty - ISBN: 978-1-61660-000-6
Written by: Kathryn Mohr
Illustrated by: Kiana Aryan

Face 2 Face - ISBN: 978-1-61660-002-0
Written by: Caroline Ster
Illustrated by: Emily Jones

Shining Through a Social Storm- ISBN: 978-1-61660-004-4
Written by: Skylar Sorkin
Illustrated by: Sydney Green

Chapter 1:
Eyes Closed, Tie Undone

Midnight. It's got to be the worst time to take a cross-country,[1] red eye flight. Saying goodbye to my friends and family didn't make it any easier, either. My wife, Anne, and I were on our way to live in New York City, and I was dreading it.

We were inside the plane, waiting for it

[1] cross-country: an airplane flight from the West Coast to the East Coast

to finish loading passengers, when I thought I'd better be smart and prepare for a long night of some of the worst sleep a person can get. I unbuckled my seat belt and made my way toward the rest rooms at the back of the plane. Fighting through a mob of people, I came to a spot in the aisle that was packed solid by folks trying to get by one another, putting bags in the crowded, overhead compartments[2] and getting situated.

As I watched the crowd, my eyes moved from face to anxious face. This was going to be a long, dreadful wait. Numerous[3] passengers remained standing, awkwardly trying to scoot around each other without the room to do so. Suddenly, out of the corner of my eye, one face seemed to reach over and turn my head in its direction.

There, just up ahead and to the left at the end of the aisle, I saw the face of a man that sent chills right through my body. I felt my jaw drop slightly open. My eyes became fixed.

[2] compartments: separate spaces in an airplane that are divided
[3] numerous: many

I forced myself through the crowd and came upon this serene-looking[4] person, eyes closed and tie undone.

I just stared at him. I scanned his entire face. *It was him for sure,* I thought.

If only I could see his right eye. Pushed by the crowd, I was forced forward and passed where he was sitting.

I stepped into the rest room and just stood there for a moment, lost in the thought of who and what I had just seen. I looked in the mirror. I splashed water on my face then took another hard look.

When I emerged from the rest room, I passed him again, glancing nonchalantly[5] back over my shoulder in his direction. His face was now turned the opposite way, his right eye clearly exposed[6]... and then I saw it—my secret, my ugly secret, one full of confusion and guilt. This unspeakable,[7] hidden secret was one of my most painful

---

[4] serene-looking: looking calm or peaceful
[5] nonchalantly: being calm and casual
[6] exposed: not hidden and able to be seen
[7] unspeakable: bad or awful

memories, confirming[8] one of my most dreaded fears.

"Allen?" I called out in what was almost a whisper. He didn't respond. I stood there for a moment, contemplating[9] whether to call out his name a second time.

Instead, I turned and walked away, all the while fighting the urge to turn around. I made my way back to my seat and sat down.

"What's wrong, Will?" Anne asked, but my mind was already far, far away.

---

[8] confirming: proving to be correct
[9] contemplating: to think seriously about something

Chapter 2:
A Terrific Place for a War

From my perspective,[10] Grove Estates, a Southern California neighborhood where my mom and I moved during my childhood, was different from all other neighborhoods. It smelled different. It sounded different. Plants and flowers full of color bloomed

[10] perspective: point of view

everywhere in sight.

Grove Estates was made up of 60 large ranch-style homes with white, picket fences. Tall, ancient[11] trees and tire swings hung in front of nearly every home. Each red brick house sat on two acre lots of just-cut, deep-green grass.

Most of the people who lived there were horse people of one kind or another—trainers, breeders,[12] show people or jockeys. Most of the houses had barns in the back to fit a whole slew[13] of horses.

Men in our neighborhood often came together in a group effort to yank a tree out of the ground or go to battle with a broken pipe of some sort. Ladies constantly[14] took food to somebody else's house as an act of hospitality. Station-wagons with teenagers hanging out of them made their way to the beach. For us kids, it was a shirts-off kind of place for the entire summer and fall (when you could still get away with it),

---

[11] ancient: very old
[12] breeder: someone who breeds animals for a job
[13] slew: a large number of something
[14] constantly: often, frequent

like right after school. As soon as we got home, *Whoosh!* the shirts were gone and we were off playing with neighborhood friends. Everyone seemed to have pop rifles, wear cowboy hats and boots, and own a dog.

Most of the streets were paved, though some weren't. None of the streets had street lamps or sidewalks, which made for mighty scary nights. As a matter of fact, on my first Halloween there, I walked down about seven houses and then came back—it was all I could take because it was pitch black.

The entire Grove Estates neighborhood shared its own water well. I thought this was great. I thought the whole neighborhood was great. I talked about it all the time, to just about everyone. I'd tell them about the families of chicken and geese you'd constantly see zigzagging all over the place, and the roosters crowing in the morning. There was also the *Klup! Klup!* of people riding their horses in the empty streets early in the morning, and the tall, rustling green trees that lined each side of the road and constantly rubbed up against each other. They would lean over to meet at the center to form a big, green tunnel.

Now, it's true that I've only lived in two neighborhoods my whole life, but still, deep down I knew this one was something pretty special.

I knew this in particular[15] because whenever somebody came over they would say something about it—every time. I loved to hear what they'd say. It was stuff like, "Hey, this is like being out in the country," or "This place makes you feel like you're in a whole other world." The one I liked the most though was when my cousin, while racing our bikes after an ice cream truck, said, "Hey, this would be a terrific place for a war."

A terrific place for a war? Now, I wasn't into fighting or anything, but I just loved the way that sounded. He was right.

---

[15] particular: for certain or specific

There were places to hide, things to throw, and tons of room to run and bike with hardly anybody in the streets.

After that, a bunch of us used to pretend like we were fighting a platoon of enemy soldiers all the time. It was so great to act tough—to fight and win...or to be killed, and then get up and go home—maybe have dinner.

If only fighting really could be that simple—that fun. If only there were no consequences[16] to fighting, I think I would have liked it. But it wasn't that simple. In fact, a fight in this very neighborhood, turned out to be one of the most complicated and confusing moments in my life.

---

[16] consequences: a result of a particular action

Chapter 3:
Wanna Play with Sumpthin'?

One summer night, my mom and I were walking straight down the middle of Grove Estates. Well, she was walking. I was riding my green, Schwinn Stingray bike with a banana seat and a slick-back tire. She was in an awful hurry. After we had walked to nearly the other side of the neighborhood, it occurred to me to ask where we were going.

"To Mrs. Heinz's house," she said.

"How come?"

"We're having a Grove Estates meeting and we're late."

"No, Mom! I don't want to do that!"

"Why not, sweetheart?"

"Well, what am I going to do? There's nothing to do!"

"You'll find something. They have a boy about your age."

"I don't want to play with someone I don't know," I whined.

The last thing I wanted to do was meet a new kid at his house. I hated that. I usually hated their toys. They seemed so boring, and I wasn't into cars. I liked them and all, but every boy my age had twenty cars. I was into Tinker Toys. The way I saw it, there weren't enough Tinker Toys in the world. Another thing—I wanted to play with toys the way I wanted to play with them. Every time you play with someone else's toys, you have to play them their way.

I was still making my case as we were on our way to the Heinz's house. "Want to bet he doesn't even have Tinker Toys?"

"I'm sure he doesn't. He's a little bit older than you—kids your age don't even play with Tinker Toys all that much."

I shot her a look that showed her that she was hitting a nerve. "Mom, you know I'm great at 'em."

"I'm not saying that's a bad thing, sweetheart, and yes, you are really good. You're my little Tinker Toy genius boy. You can create objects those Tinker Toy people never even dreamed."

This is going to be boring, I thought to myself. "Well, I'm just going to stay with you for the whole night then," I proclaimed.

"Let's just see how it goes, Will."

Mom rang the doorbell and Mrs. Heinz came to the door, swinging it open like she was trying to yank it off its hinges. It scared me half to death.

"Well, you must be Mrs. Francisco!" bellowed Mrs. Heinz. She was a large, bulbous[17] woman with red hair and glasses and a big flower dress.

"Hello, Mrs. Heinz, it's nice to meet you. Thank you for inviting us to your meeting."

"Of course! Come in, come in!" she exclaimed. "Well, who's this young man?" I could just feel the *oh-brother* look I must have had on my face.

"This is my son, Will," Mom answered.

"Well hello, Will. How old is a young man like yourself?"

There was a perfectly good one-syllable answer to this question and I saw no reason to go on and on.

"Nine."

"Nine? Well, we're so happy to have you both here and part of our special, special neighborhood. It's nice to see a boy from La

---

[17] bulbous: round in shape

Monde Road all the way out here in enemy territory," Mrs. Heinz said with a laugh.

"Enemy territory?" my mom asked.

"Oh, it's just some unwritten rule that the boys on this side of Orangewood have nothing to do with the boys on the other side of Orangewood and vice versa. Isn't that silly, Will?" said Mrs. Heinz.

"Yes, ma'am."

"Yes. Now are you ready to go meet my Allen? He's a youngster, just like you."

"Well, I think I'm just going to hang out with my mom tonight—"

She yanked me by the hand and led me to a closed door. She knocked and swung it open all in the same motion, and I was in.

Much to my shock, Allen wasn't a kid at all. He was like twelve or something.

"Allen, this is Will Francisco. Say hi to him."

"Hi," he replied, without looking up from what he was drawing. It was a cheerful sounding two-note[18] "hi" where the first note is higher than the second. When my mom and Mrs. Heinz left, I just stood there.

It took him a couple of minutes to finish his drawing. Finally, he looked up and asked, "You wanna play with sumpthin'?"

"What'ya got?" I asked timidly.

"All kinds of stuff. Look at that." He pointed behind me to a huge track for his electric cars which sat upon a complex system of Tinker Toys. It went up three full levels. It had bridges and hills and turns and twists. It was awesome.

Allen took out his cars and placed them on the track. It was so cool to see these cars going around a track in the air!

Then Allen said, "You want to take the whole thing apart and change it around?"

"You mean the Tinker Toys?"

"Yeah, the whole thing. We'll do whatever you want."

I took hold of the Tinker Toys and

---

[18] two-note: when words are said by changing your voice as you would in music going from one music note to the next note on the scale

started to pull them apart. Allen jumped in enthusiastically. We yanked and pulled. We played as hard and fast as our hands would let us, trying to get as much of this fun in as we possibly could. His hands seemed better with the Tinker Toys than mine. I couldn't keep up, but he didn't seem to care that I was lagging behind. He treated me like a real buddy. Like we were partners in rebuilding this thing. Like we had known each other for a zillion years.

My shyness went away. I spoke to him freely. I wasn't afraid to make mistakes. We fell to the ground laughing hysterically. In just two hours, Allen had become my best friend of all time.

When the door opened, I don't think I'd ever been so unhappy to see my mom in my life.

"Are you ready to go, sweetheart?" she said.

"Aw, c'mon Mom. Can't you talk for a little while longer?"

"No, it's already getting late. We need

to go home and have dinner."

"Can't they feed us?"

"No," she replied, horrified by my rude[19] suggestion.

"You're more than welcome to stay," said Mrs. Heinz. "I can put something on right now—shouldn't take more than a couple of minutes and we'd love to have you."

"Are you sure?" Mom asked. I looked at Allen excitedly. He casually shrugged his shoulders with a *sounds-ok-to-me* face.

* * *

Screech-Slam went the screen door as Allen and I bounded outside.

"What'ya got?" I asked.

"Tons. Take your pick," he said. I stood in the middle of his backyard, just taking it all in, and not knowing which direction to go first. He had a cool mound of dirt with a bunch of army men laying around. He had a

---

[19] rude: obnoxious comment

hose that stretched across the yard that he obviously used to gun down the army men. He had balls of all different colors and sizes here and there. A big surfboard leaned against the house. An old dog twitched his eyebrows when I walked by, completely uninterested by my presence. There was also a bike frame with no tires hanging upside down, and stuck between two vices in the middle of the patio.

"What's that?" I asked.

"My dad and I are building a bike for me—gonna paint it gun-metal gray. My dad thinks we ought to paint 'Heinz' along the side like I'm a real, live bike maker, but I don't know about that."

"That's awesome!" I said, and I just stared at it for awhile.

"Want to see my secret hideaway?" he asked.

Over in the corner of his yard stood a tree which had no branches or leaves from the trunk up to about five feet up. From that point to the top, the tree was covered in a dense cloud of branches and leaves. The tree's shape mushroomed out, making it look like a giant, green ball. "Come on," Allen said.

Arriving underneath the leaves, we looked up and my eyes could barely take it all in. On every branch there were ropes zigzagging, wood planks joining branches together, old couch cushions, gnarly-looking pillows, books, and toy army men tied up everywhere.

"Wow," I said in fascinated disbelief.

"Come on up," Allen said, and with that, he scurried up that tree faster than I could notice how he had done it. "Just grab this here, put one foot there, and pull. You'll be okay."

Once at the top, the leaves were so thick that I couldn't believe how hidden we were. "Your parents don't know this is here?"

"Yeah, they do. I just call it a secret

hideaway because no one can see you."

"Well, it's still awesome."

"You want to know what is a secret?" Allen pointed up to the back corner of the tree where there was a hole among the leaves. "That. C'mon."

I followed Allen way up to the hole. "Are you hungry?" he asked me. I gave him an, "I have no idea what you are getting at" look. Allen moved the leaves aside to reveal a telephone pole. He smacked it a few times.

"See this? We can climb down this telephone pole just a few feet to the wall that goes behind all the homes on Court Lane. About three homes down, Mr. Kleinhoff has an old stable that sits at an angle on his property. We can step onto the top of the stable, walk along it to the other side, jump back down onto the wall, and we'll be standing directly inside Mrs. Droesser's orange tree—full of oranges as fat as your head."

"Is it dangerous?" I asked.

"Well...it's fun," he said. "If you don't want to do it, we don't have to."

"No—that's okay. Let's do it," I said. He turned. I gulped.

"Okay. Just reach around the side of the pole and you'll feel a metal thingy sticking out of it. They go all the way down on both sides. So just follow it down 'til you get to the wall. Get on and follow me, okay?"

"Okay."

"You can go slowly," he reminded me.

"Okay."

He took hold of the pole and started down. "Oh, and watch out for the dogs," he added.

Now he tells me. I made my way down onto the wall where he was waiting. Many places along the walls were thick enough to get good footing, even double footing at times, and the trees along the wall were helpful as you walked along.

"Try to be real quiet," Allen said. "We

don't want dogs around." None of them can jump high enough to bite you, but it's nerve-racking as all get out when they try."

It was dusk, and I thought how cool it was that we must've looked like commandos lurking against the gray and orange sky. Just ahead, Allen held up his hand and I stopped. He pointed straight ahead at the stable on Mr. Kleinhoff's property. I nodded. He stepped up to the top and waved me forward. He waited for me to get there then he took my arm and pulled me up. We walked along the top real sneaky-like to the other end, where we jumped down to the wall below. Sure enough, there we were, smack dab in the middle of an orange tree.

"Check this out," he said quietly. Allen pulled an orange from one branch and handed it to me. Man o' man, they were huge.

My mom always peeled my oranges for me, I thought. *Maybe I should ask Allen to peel it for me. No. It's time to be a man.*

"Wait a minute," I heard him say. Looking up, I saw that he was focused on the yard of the house next door. He moved some leaves out of the way. "That's my sister!" he said in a loud whisper.

I parted the leaves myself and saw what he saw. There stood a girl and a boy holding hands.

"Watch this," Allen said.

Trying his best to sound like a man, he called out, "WHY, THIS IS THE THIRD BOY THIS WEEK!"

I yanked back my hands, letting my little hole of leaves close up. Then I heard his sister give the most ear-piercing yell: "ALLEN THOMAS HEINZ!"

"C'MON!" Allen screamed, and like a bolt of light, he darted along the wall toward Mr. Kleinhoff's stable. He bounded up to the top and I followed after him, scared half to death. He ran along the top of the stable and I did too. I came across a skylight, jumped over it and *CRASH!*—the wood below me gave way and I began to fall through the boards. Frantically, I reached up, trying to grab onto anything I could, but there I was, hanging onto a support beam that felt like it was going to break. Down below stood eight horses in separate stalls, and each one was startled.

"Help!" I cried out. I was hanging over the middle of one stall while the horses were locked up in stalls on either side. I could have let go and fallen straight down, but it looked way too far.

Just then, I heard the stable doors open at the far end. It was Allen. "Help!" I said again when I saw him. Allen ran directly to where I was, put out both arms and said, "You're going to have to let go."

"There's no way!" I said with a whimper.

Allen spoke deliberately and a bit slower than one might expect, considering the situation. "Yes, there is. I saw the lights come on in Mr. Kleinhoff's house. He's going to be coming through the other door any second. You better let go right now or we're in big trouble."

"I can't."

"Trust me, man. I won't let you get hurt."

On faith and faith alone, I let go. Clinched fingers opened. I fell for what seemed like a hundred miles—*BAM!* I landed on Allen and we fell together. "Let's go!" he said.

We picked ourselves up and ran like crazy to the door at the far end. As quietly and quickly as he could, Allen closed the door behind us, then we bolted. Up onto the wall we scrambled, pulling and tugging as hard as we could. "My fault, my fault," Allen kept saying over and over.

We heard Mr. Kleinhoff open the door and start talking to his horses, "What's going on in here, ladies? What the…"

By this time, we were running along the back wall towards Allen's house, while every dog in the neighborhood erupted in blood-curling howls. In the distance we heard the stable door open. Then Mr. Kleinhoff yelled, "Hey! Who is that? Get back here!"

We passed three homes, climbed up the telephone pole to the hole in the tree, climbed down and dropped *C'bam-style* onto the grass in Allen's backyard. Then we laughed our brains out, chuckling, "No way! No way! No way!"

At that moment, Mrs. Heinz slid open the screen door and said, "You boys must be starving. Who wants an orange?"

Back to the ground we went, each of us holding our sides. I conked my head against the grass, but I didn't care. Man, it felt good to laugh that hard.

* * *

Later, after dinner, it was time to go home.

"Well, see ya," Allen said.
"See ya."

As we walked home, I told my mom how much fun I had hanging out with Allen. She assured me that if I wanted to, I could see Allen anytime. Somehow, though, "anytime" just never came. I ended up making friends with some guys from my part of the neighborhood and spent most of my time hanging out with them.

I only saw Allen a few times after that night. My mom I were driving by and we saw him raking leaves in his front yard. He waved and I waved back.

Once, I'm pretty sure I saw his face in a car as he drove by my house. I'm not sure, really, but I think it was him.

Another time I passed him on my bike while riding to 7-Eleven. He was riding with friends going the other way. I gave him one of those raised-chin *hellos*. I'm not sure he saw it, though.

* * *

A year later I saw him again, walking by the front of my elementary school. I was on my bike across the street. We noticed each other, but neither of us waved. No reason, really—We just didn't do it.

I guess it was at that time when I realized we had forever lost the possibility of hanging out again. Too much time had passed. Although I still really liked and admired Allen, it was okay—and I don't know why it was okay, really. I guess I just got use to hanging around with the kids on my street, even though I liked them a lot less than I did Allen. Plus, my mom said she didn't want to search "all over the world" to find me and didn't want me crossing Orangewood. It's just one of those things that happen, I guess.

But I must say, in all my years, I had never met anybody as kind and generous as Allen Heinz, or anybody who acted so interested in being my friend, or anybody who seemed to want nothing more than to make sure I had a good time. And man, I had a good time.

Chapter 4: The Gang

Straight down the middle of Grove Estates was one of the main streets that seemed to define who would be your friend and who wouldn't. Although I don't know for sure, it's impossible to believe that the other side of the neighborhood was filled with as many characters as ours.

First, there was Lars, my fun, always-bruised, hyperactive friend. He was 100% out of control 100% of the time. He was German and proud as all get out. He even had a German bike. Now, none of us could tell if his bike was actually faster than ours, or if it was his hyperactivity that allowed him to pump his pedals twice as fast as us. But one thing was for sure—when it was time to race, Lars was already at the end popping wheelies[20] waiting for us.

Even when he was pulling Bertram, "better known as Berty," his handicapped younger brother in a wagon attached to his bike, he was still faster than the rest of us. It was probably because Lars only understood fast, eye-bulging, tongue-wagging

[20] wheelies: to lift the front wheel of the bicycle you are riding and balance on the back wheel

speed. What I could never understand was why, day after day, Berty would continue to allow himself to be yanked around Grove Estates on the verge of a total, skin-scraping and utter disaster.

When we saw Berty, he usually looked utterly terrified about the ride. His tiny hands death-gripped the edges of his red Radio Flyer wagon. His eyes became twice their size, and both corners of his mouth pushed straight down while his jaw jetted in toward his neck. You would've thought he was riding a roller coaster straight off of a cliff.

Every once in a while, Lars would spill Berty. With blinding speed, he would skid his bike to a halt, drop it with total abandon, pick up Berty without caring whether he had him by the head or something else, throw him in the wagon, and off they would go again. They would easily pass us, of course. Eventually, it dawned on me that the only person more out of control than Lars was Berty.

On occasion, Lars' recklessness got him into trouble. Once, while leaving my house, he ran right in front of a mail truck and *C'bam*—ol' Lars was airborne.

That day I also gained a little insight as to how their mom must've felt about having a difficult son like Lars. She came out of the house, saw Lars lying there, and ran to his side before dashing back in to call an ambulance without a tear. It was like she knew it was coming.

Next, was Billy Holberg who was definitely a little boy; however, at the time we weren't so sure. He looked less like a kid, and more like a stunted, bald, moldy-skinned, old person who you would be afraid to touch. He was very skinny with stringy, blonde hair and not much of it. His shoulders dropped straight down when his hands reached for his pockets.

Billy lived next door to us and had a slew of sisters, all of whom strongly disliked him. They were always arguing and fighting about something.

Rebecka

Then there was Rebecka Hitchcock who lived on Otter Road. She was into girl power and all that. She wanted us to call her Beck. I didn't like that. Your name is your name, the way I see it. She was exactly our age, but talking to her was like having a conversation with a college student. She used big words. She thought strange thoughts. She wore plaid wool skirts, blouses that buttoned all the way to the neck, and sometimes wore wire glasses. She liked knee socks and Converse shoes. She had a boy's blue Schwinn, which she rarely rode. She sort of had her own angle on everything, a girls-can-do-anything-boys-can-do sort of thing. It maddened me, but entranced me at the same time. I loved her. We all did.

What's more, Beck had the one physical characteristic that drove all of us out of our minds. She was ambidextrous,[21] and somehow it seemed to support her angle on life because no boy could do what she could. Her favorite way to display this ability was to write with both hands at the same time. That was my favorite, too. We'd all gather around her and go, *"Oooh."* This only seemed to heighten my feelings for her.

Then there were Karl and Ducky, twins who lived across the street and one house over from me, next door to Lars and Berty. Karl was a tall, thin kid and rode an awesome red, shiny Royce Union.

---

[21] ambidextrous: to be able to use either hand equally well

Ducky, on the other hand, had a thicker build with the best belly laugh ever. He had this contagious laugh that could get all us laughing and we wouldn't even know what was funny. We all loved him.

There was also Candy, who always wore pink and had one heck of a throwing arm, which she used all the time. She'd conk you on the head with a rock or ball or toy or something before you even knew she was mad at you, and her accuracy was remarkable. She could even pop you while riding her spray-painted, pink Schwinn.

There was never a question of whether or not she'd hit you—if she wanted to, you were hit. Once, she hit me square in the nose with a tree branch. After I bled for three hours, my mom started to panic so I was rushed to a hospital where I had my nose cauterized.[22] I'm still not sure what that is. Still, it hurt like mad and it was all because of Candy's strange tendency to pick up the closest thing and hurl it at you.

Another thing Candy could do was lie. I guess when you do something enough, you tend to get good at it—and boy, was she good. She could be real sneaky-like too.

You'd ask, "Candy, was that you?"

"Who?"

"Who did that?"

And she would reply very innocently, "How should I know who did that? I wasn't even there."

Responses like that usually threw me. At ten, I couldn't make heads or tails out of what she was saying, but I knew something wasn't quite right.

---

[22] cauterized: a procedure to stop persistent bleeding from a small vein or artery usually in the front of the nose

There was Richie Webber, a kid who had everything. You name it, he had it. He even had things you never heard of—in threes. He liked Quicksilver shirts, so his mom bought him 60. In fact, he would get two new t-shirts every week. We'd go over to his house all the time and just stare at his closet like we were in a museum. Richie was also so short that his dad bought him a midget-sized yellow, ten-speed Schwinn. It was awesome. Nothing made a kid like me feel more like a teenager than pedaling a ten speed. He really didn't care that it was a miniature; he was absolutely thrilled to be riding anything other than a regular old, normal-looking bike.

One time when Ducky got a mini-bike, Richie asked for one too, but he wanted a three wheeler instead—so he got one. I asked him on several occasions if I could ride it and he'd always say, "No." One day, however, he finally gave in and let me. It took about five seconds for me to lose control of it and crash through the Webber's wooden fence. Richie was strangely calm about it. He just looked at all the splintered wood lying around, and then walked inside to eat one of his daily chocolate pudding cups.

About ten minutes later, his dad came home. When Mr. Webber saw what I had done, his head started quivering and kind of vibrating or something. He stomped inside, and through the window I saw him ask Richie what had happened. Without taking his eyes off the TV, Richie told him. I just stood there next to the rubble.

Then Mr. Webber busted out of the house with nails and hammer in hand. It was a very strange moment in my life. Somehow I felt the need to stand there next to Mr. Webber as he furiously attempted to repair the fence. It was just me and him in his backyard, not talking to each other. I knew he didn't want me there. I knew he was angry with me, but for some reason I can't explain I couldn't bring myself to leave until he was done. Richie never came out of the house.

These were my friends. The best friends a kid could ever want (except for Allen Heinz) and all were discovered in one-half of a neighborhood. Once, we fantasized about calling ourselves a gang and soon we would get our chance.

Chapter 5:
Mark and the Muscle

At our age most kids had an idol or hero in life. We would talk about it all the time. Mine were Kobe Bryant and Shaquille O'Neal, the best 1-2 punch in NBA history.

Lars's was Jeff Gordon.

Beck's was Bobby Kennedy.[23]

---

[23] Bobby Kenndy: A democratic Senator from New York and noted civil rights activist and advisor to his older brother, President John F. Kennedy. He was U.S. Attorney General from 1961 to 1964 and assassinated while running for president in 1968.

But for Trev Jones, the muscular, thirteen-year-old, chip-on-his-shoulder kid, who lived down the street, it was Mark Matts. Who was Mark Matts? He was the scrawny 14-year-old who lived just across the street from Trev. I have to say that, in defense of Trev, Mark was every bit as interesting as Trev made him out to be. Mark was a mysterious and wise, philosophy-spouting kid with quite a penchant[24] for trouble—a real spiritual guru[25] riding a purple Schwinn.

Sometimes he'd sit and interpret the Book of Revelation,[26] or he'd get us together at night and tell us stories where somebody always showed up missing one hand. He liked to speak slowly and use big words. We would all sit there and get a bad case of the heebie jeebies.

---

[24] penchant: something you do often
[25] guru: someone who knows a lot of information about a certain topic
[26] Book of Revelation: the last book in the New Testament of the Bible which describes a story how the world is going to end

Mark's talents seemed limitless. For one, he dug a ditch that weaved throughout his mom's half-acre property, creating a kind of maze effect. It had rooms and hallways and stuff. Then he put boards on top of the ditches, covering them with dirt to make a long tunnel.

From ground level, you couldn't tell there was a tunnel there at all. True, you don't normally see underground tunnels from above ground, but nevertheless, we were utterly fascinated by this invisible thing only we knew was there. We rode by it all the time—just to look at it. We'd only speak about it to each other though. Not even our parents knew. Even if there's no reason, some things just have to be secret.

At night, we would go down into the tunnel. Mark would take frogs, his guitar, and potato bugs in a jar, and by candlelight he'd tell us all of the weird stuff he could think of at the moment. We'd be mesmerized.[27]

---

[27] mesmerized: captivated, extremely interested, have powerful effect

Another time, he built a two-story structure in his backyard. It felt like it was going to fall over any second, but it was impressive as all get out.

He could cook, too. He would make us anything we wanted. Imagine that—a house full of ten-year-olds being fed by a kid just a few years older. That was the strangest thing to me. It seemed to me that when there was cooking to be done, it should be by a mom or a dad wearing an apron that read something like, "World's Greatest Dad." The real kicker was that we would all be sitting there, eating omelets or something, and listening to Mark's favorite rock band, Crash Burn. Metal, he'd call it. Man, it freaked me out, but was also kind of liberating[28] at the same time. I don't know.

Around Mark, Trev always acted like the ultimate protector.[29] It was sort of the way Chubaka acted around Hans Solo in Star Wars. He was fascinated by everything about

---

[28] liberating: to free someone of a feeling or something
[29] protector: to defend someone

Mark. Mark wore his greasy, sandy-brown hair parted on the side and combed to hang down over one eye, and so did Trev. Mark got a ten-speed, and so did Trev. Mark would call us dweebs. Trev would too.

I don't know who started it first, but they both spit like they couldn't stand the taste of their own saliva—like after every sentence or something—sometimes right in the middle of one. Being barefoot around them was no good. Once I even saw Mark spit in his house. I am pretty sure he had forgotten where he was, although he didn't let on to that fact.

Even though the spitting was kind of disgusting, it also looked kind of cool. So I tried it for awhile, but I couldn't develop a style. Mark and Trev would be talking to you and then suddenly whisk one over your shoulder. Me? I had to turn around and kind of drop one straight down. It just didn't feel right, so I gave it up. All the other guys kept it up for awhile too, until they also seemed to forget about it.

Lars kept spitting, though. So did Berty and I have to admit it, he could spit an incredible loogie. With a curled tongue, his chest would expand to twice its size and *thoooo!*—it would land, like, way over there. Maybe it was the fact that he was sitting down. I should've tried that.

Because Mark did so many weird things, and also because Trev was so big, Trev was always having to protect Mark—at least that is what he said. I didn't believe him though—until one day.

That's the day Mark got into a fight at the 7-Eleven with Allen Heinz, the one guy Mark wanted to punch more than anyone, and the guy who could've been my best friend. Allen pulled "a zillion" of Mark's hairs out, and afterward, Trev was determined that Allen would suffer his revenge[30] for hurting Mark. Unfortunately, he recruited[31] me and my friends to help him.

---

[30] revenge: to get even
[31] recruited: to persuade people to join a group

He brought us all together in the tunnel and told us what he wanted.

"Here, in this part of Grove Estates, we do not let things like this happen to one of our own," Trev preached, "especially when it's by a loser like Allen Heinz."

As far as I knew, the guys from Grove Estates didn't have a history of fighting and bullying,[32] but Trev made it sound like they did.

"After all that Mark has done for us, we've got no choice, but to back him up." He was really steamed.

"What do we have to do?" Billy asked anxiously as he shifted from sitting Indian-style to sitting on both knees.

"Mark's inside his house and he's got a whole plan laid out. All you have to do is follow it to a 'T' and Allen will be dust, man." *Spit.* "Now what I'm going to do is go inside and get Mark and he'll tell you about it. Hold on."

---

[32] bullying: to threaten or frighten someone who is smaller or weaker

Trev skirted out of our meeting space, in the tunnel, and disappeared into Mark's house. I was scared. Ganging up on Allen, and actually hitting him or something, was the last thing I wanted to do. None of the other guys seemed too scared about it, though. In fact, everybody seemed pretty pumped up.

Soon Mark and Trev entered the tunnel and Trev began to talk excitedly. "Okay, listen up. This is about as serious as it gets, guys." All eyes went to Mark. He sat there very still.

"I have a plan," he said stoically, as his face was illuminated[33] eerily[34] by a candle he held a few inches from his chin. "Allen has agreed to meet me over where the paved road turns to dirt. We're going to have it out once and for all, only I've got a surprise for him." This would be where Mark would reveal some incredibly sinister[35] plan that would make him look like a genius.

"Right alongside the road is a long row of bushes where you will hide. As

---

[33] illuminated: lit up by a light
[34] eerily: strange and frightening
[35] sinister: making you feel that something evil or dangerous is happening

soon as you see Allen get off his bike, you're going to pelt him with dirt clods that have stickers inside of them. I'm going to make them and they're going to leave a mark. Then, as soon as he starts to run, Trev is going to come riding out of nowhere and ram him with his bike. Once he falls, I'm going to let him have it."

Hmmmm, I thought to myself. *The plan had clearly taken some thought, but it still didn't seem all that great. I mean, besides Candy, what if we all missed him? Couldn't we just as easily hit him with water balloons or something? Did it have to be so painful? I attend church, for cryin' out loud. How mad could they really be?*

"I have a question," I said timidly. "Do we have to hit him with things that hurt so much?"

"Well, what do you want to hit him with instead?" Trev remarked mockingly, "Water balloons?" Everyone started laughing in my face.

"No, I don't know, man. Just maybe something else is all."

"Forget that garbage, dude. It's going hurt and hurt bad!" At this, everyone else cheered. Lars's face became scrunched up and he nearly began foaming from the mouth. Karl clapped his hands. Ducky and Richie smacked each other around a little bit.

"Now are we going to do this, or what?" Trev said. "You guys are always talking about being a gang. Here's your chance!"

Everybody erupted with exuberance.[36] They jeered and cheered and raised their fists. I didn't, but they did. Like it or not, I was in.

---

[36] exuberance: full of energy and excitement

Chapter 6:
A Change of Plans

A couple of days later, my mom was going to a Wednesday night church service and she had decided to drag me along. It's usually a kind of boring experience because the youth group is a fraction of the kids who show up on Sunday mornings.

The kids who come on Wednesday night are typically not the same group of kids that I hang out with on Sunday. Nobody really knows each other. We're usually all different ages, and there's only one teacher for all of us, so we're all slapped together in one group. You should hear us singing the songs at song time, It's anything but glorious. Of course, I'm no help. In all the time I've been there I haven't sung one, single, solitary note.

The class ended and all the kids ran out to find their parents. I went out to the front of the church, looking for my mom who was usually chatting in the same place, but I didn't see her. I waited a bit longer, but still no sign of Mom. *Maybe she's still in the church praying with some lady or something*, I thought.

So I walked into the sanctuary.[37] Nobody was there. It was just row after row of empty pews,[38] a stage, and a pulpit that had an uncomfortable silence about it.

---

[37] sanctuary: a room where religious services take place
[38] pews: a long wooden seat in a house of worship

The whole sanctuary was peaceful. It dawned[39] on me that maybe this was an opportunity to get myself out of this fight. Church. Silence. I'm all alone. It had to be a sign.

I sat down in the second pew. I thought about kneeling, but then I thought, *Naw, this is good enough*. "Dear God," I said, "I figure with me all alone in this church and all, I was thinking that maybe you'll really listen to my prayer. You see, I really can't do this fighting business. I don't want to fight Allen, but I know I can't just not show up. I could never face the guys again. Please God, help me make a good decision."

"Mr. Francisco," bellowed a large voice. God?

I looked up. It was Pastor Shugart, the senior pastor. He was a thick, short guy, with a large, dark mustache that had a big patch of gray in it. The mustache looked like it didn't know if it was coming or going.

---

[39] dawned: when an idea comes to you for the first time

"Oh, hello Pastor Shugart," I said hoping he would just pass me by.

"You okay?" he asked. He reached out, shook my hand, and sat down.

"Oh, yeah, I'm fine," I said. "I was just praying to the almighty God," I replied, hoping to impress him.

He didn't say anything. I had to fill in the silence. "You know, about things here and there."

"Sounds like you have some things on your mind. Do you want to talk about it?"

"Not really. It's a really long story. I have a decision I have to make and what I really hope happens is that God, in his great Godliness, can just get me out of having to make the decision at all."

"I see," said Pastor Shugart. "Well, what I have learned is that God rarely gets you out of having to make a decision, I'm afraid. **But just as a general rule of thumb, if you ever have to make a decision between two different things, the hardest one is usually the right one.**"

That was the last piece of news I wanted to hear. I needed out of this predicament. But if I was to follow his rule of thumb, I was going to have to tell the fellas I wasn't going to fight.

A couple of weeks went by and none of us had heard from Trev or Mark. In the first couple of days, the bunch of us talked about it a lot, but after a while, it seemed like everybody just kind of forgot.

This couldn't have made me happier. It seemed like my prayers were being answered and this whole thing would just go away.

Still, it was on my mind. I really liked Allen.

Friday night came around, and still there was no word from either Trev or Mark. Then, the doorbell rang, and something told me that it was Trev. I heard my mom call me. I walked slowly toward the doom.

"Hi, Will, can you come out?"

"Um, I think we're about to eat."

"C'mon. It'll just take a minute." We walked away from the house and out onto the street. He spoke from on top of his bike.

"Okay. Meet us tomorrow at 11:30 where the road turns to dirt. Mark will give us instructions then. Okay?" I nodded hesitantly.[40] "OKAY?" he snapped.

"Yeah."

"Hey, you gettin' scared or something?" I thought hard about his question for a second or two.

"I'll see you tomorrow," I said. I started walking back toward the house. Trev rode off.

11:25 A.M. came the following day and the pack of us rode to the proposed battlefield together. Much to my dismay, everyone was all drummed up for the event. Lars, Richie, Karl, Ducky, Candy, and Billy couldn't get there fast enough. *Okay, take it easy*, I thought to myself.

I soon discovered that Berty wasn't with us. Beck wasn't either, and at one point

---

[40] hesitantly: to stop and pause before doing or saying anything.

a thought went through my mind that maybe I would refuse to fight as well. Unfortunately, there was no way these guys were going to let me back out of this. So I rode on without a word, my stomach in my throat.

When we got to the meeting spot, Mark and Trev were waiting on their bikes in the middle of the road.

"Hey, guys," Mark said. "There's been a change in plans." Suddenly I had a burst of hope, a real feeling that everything was going to be okay.

"Instead of everyone being in the bushes, I'm going to keep Billy, Richie, and of course Candy, here to peg Allen. I'm also going to keep Ducky here and use him as a human shield if I need it." At this, Ducky pounded his chest with his massively squishy fist. "Now, I'm going to station Karl over by the entrance to Grove Estates with the dirt clods, so he can fire them on Allen if he tries to run away. Will, you are going to be positioned over by the strawberry field because Allen could try to escape through there, too. I'm going to keep Lars here with me and use him as a runner in case I need to relay any messages to Karl and Will—he's by far the fastest way to get any word to them."

"Aw, man. I want to throw dirt clods, too!" Lars insisted.

"Don't worry about it, man. You'll throw plenty." Lars pumped both fists and scrunched up his nose.

"Also, to make sure everything goes perfectly, I have a few friends coming to back me up." Although I had heard what he said, I was so filled with fear that I didn't really consider what that might mean.

We were given our dirt clods in plastic bags and were told to take our positions.

* * *

The strawberry patch ran alongside Grove Estates in one of the most remote[41]

---

[41] remote: isolated, far from other places.

parts of the neighborhood. It lay way over on the far end of Otter Road where the last Grove Estates houses stood. It was also where Beck lived. This location seemed the best possible place for me. There was nobody around, and I saw no reason why Allen would be coming in from this direction. He lived the opposite way down the road. I was really happy that I wasn't right where the action would be—there was a real chance that I wouldn't see any fighting at all.

Gathering a few strawberries, I climbed a tree and waited there, my plastic bag of dirt clods tied to my wrist.

Half an hour went by and I was still sitting there. I heard nothing. I saw nothing. I was beginning to think that I had put in enough time, and that no one would hold it against me if I just went home.

Then there was the other side to my idea. Maybe if I stayed for a bit longer I could say that I had eagerly waited for a chance to get involved in the fighting, that I had hung on until the bitter end just so I could get a piece of Allen Heinz. Maybe Beck would come out of her house and see me here. Thinking that she'd be pretty darn impressed with me willing to fight and all, I switched to a cooler way of sitting. You know, just in case.

Ten more minutes went by—nothing. I stared down the road at the illusion that the heat of the day had on the dirt—you know, when it looks like waves are coming up off the ground? Then, right where I was looking, I saw Lars rounding the corner toward me like a blur. He was moving like he'd been shot out of a cannon. His face looked like he had just seen a ghost.

I waved and called to him from the tree. Lars skidded to a stop below me, knocking over my bike in the process.

"Will!" Lars screamed desperately, "Allen showed up with four of his cousins, and two of Mark's friends came, and Trev and Ducky got into it; then, they all started fighting and they are really throwing punches! Ducky got kicked in the stomach, Mark has a bloody nose, Trev hit somebody over the head with a rock, and everybody is bleeding. It was terrible and I'm going home!"

"When, when, when did this happen?" I stuttered.

"It just all happened right now! Get out of here, man. You're going to get killed!" A feeling like I had never felt before came over me—anxiety filled with absolute terror. I felt completely out of control. It was the most powerful sensation of any kind I had ever experienced in my life.

Lars didn't wait for me. He took off like a bolt.[42] He was out of sight in a matter of seconds. I climbed down to another branch, then lept ten feet to the ground. I got on my bike and started riding, but to tell you the truth—I was so confused that I didn't know which way to go. I was overcome with panic.

---

[42] bolt: sudden or quick

Dead ahead of me appeared the old, unused, white-stucco horse stables that stood in a big plot of long, green grass. I raced over to them, dropped my bike outside one of the stables, and ran inside. As I ran in, I looked out the window-like opening of the stable at another matching stable about 40 feet in front of where I was. It was then that I saw Allen arriving at the other stable, breathing heavily. He squatted, leaning against the corner of it, facing the opposite direction from me.

I ran over to the door of the stable, looked down, found a jagged piece of cement, picked it up, and fired it in Allen's direction.

Slowly, all sound turned off in my head. All feeling left my feet. My lungs filled up with lead. I felt myself slowly blink. All the while my heart beat like a piston in my chest.

I followed the flight of the rock for a mile in the bright, blue sky.

The rock soared, then smashed against the side of Allen's face, catching him right above the eye. He collapsed behind the stable with only his motionless feet remaining in view.

In disbelief, I watch for a moment before dropping to the ground myself. I put my head against my knees and put my arms against the sides of my face. I wept. I shook as I did. The muscles in my face pulled and strained. "What did I do, what did I do, what did I do?" My stomach turned and twisted and wrenched. I watched my tears stream to the ground, just inches from my face.

I finally gained the courage to look again to see if Allen's feet were still visible behind the stable. They weren't. He had left. I layed back down in the cool, muddy grass and cried some more. I didn't care that I might be found. I deserved punishment—the cruelest kind.

What had made me do this to a boy I really liked? A strange weariness came over me. With my face in the mud I lay there, unable to move.

One hour went by.

A fly landed loudly on my cheek by my ear. The wind picked up and my arms grew goose bumps, but my muscles had yet to awaken. My body felt like dead weight.

Another hour went by.

Finally, with my very first headache, I slowly got up and stumbled my way over to my bike. I walked it onto the road, got on, and started the slow ride back home. On the way, I had strange feelings. Many thoughts raced through my brain. I wondered if I would be changed by the day's events. I certainly felt different. I felt violent…but one thing I knew for sure—what had happened on that day would always remain my secret.

The only time I ever saw Allen again was in my memories and in my prayers—I'd picture him then, too. However, he was never really hurt in my reveries[43]—just happy, well, and smiling.

---

[43] reveries: dreaming or thinking about pleasant things

Chapter 7:
Good Luck

The plane was dark. Most everyone seemed asleep. Anne uncoiled herself from her curled-up sleeping position and opened one eye to find me wide-eyed, biting on my thumbnail and staring straight ahead.

"What are you doing?" she asked as her voice cracked from not sleeping well. I looked at her for a moment. "Just thinking," I said distantly.[44]

"Are we almost there?"

I looked at my watch. "I think we have about an hour to go."

"An hour? I'm going to go back to sleep then."

"Yeah. Go ahead."

An hour to go. I noticed my knee was beginning to bounce up and down. I think my body realized before my mind did that, with just a little time left in the flight, it was now or never—I had to talk to Allen.

I leaned into the aisle and noticed a light on, right about the seat where Allen was sitting. I got up and made my way through the quiet plane toward him.

Allen was there, awake and reading a magazine. I approached him. He looked up at me.

"Allen?"

"Yes?" he replied, obviously unaware of

---

[44] distantly: when your mind is far away thinking of something

who I was.

"I'm…um…We used to uh…Do you remember back in…?"

"Will Francisco?" he half-questioned, half-announced with a calming smile.

"Yes! How are you doing, Allen?"

He greeted me warmly so I knelt there, leaning against a seat across the aisle and we began to talk without hesitation. We talked about his parents, my parents, his old house, his job that takes him all across the country, his wife, kids, my job, Anne, our move to New York.

As we reminisced,[45] I learned an amazing fact. After Allen and his family moved away from Grove Estates to a nearby neighborhood at the end of that year. Allen, Trev, and Mark ultimately became friends. They spent quite a bit of time together in high school until Trev and his parents moved to Northern California and sadly, Mark died of cancer[46] when he was just 17.

---

[45] reminisced: to talk or think about pleasant events in your past
[46] cancer: a disease that grows cells that are not normal

I could only tell him a little about my friends. Candy was living with her husband in Sacramento where she trained show horses; Richie still lived with his parents in Grove Estates, and I never did see Lars and Berty again after their family moved to Canada. I told him that I had heard that Berty finally succumbed[47] to the disease that had put him in the wheelchair. He was 21. Everybody else, as far as I knew, just moved away from the neighborhood at one time or another.

We talked there for about 45 minutes until the flight attendant asked us all to prepare for landing.

We told each other how good it was to meet up again, and wished each other well. After that, I returned to my seat.

About 20 minutes later, the plane landed and came to a complete stop. People pulled themselves up and scrambled to grab their things and get off the plane. I found myself stalling, but soon Anne became

---

[47] succumbed: to become very ill or die

impatient and insisted that I push to get out as fast as possible.

Finally, we made it into the airport terminal. As we approached the main corridor, something continued to eat at me. We turned right and walked down about 50 feet before I stopped and turned around.

"What's the matter?" Anne asked me.

Scanning the crowd, I spotted Allen, walking down the same corridor in the opposite direction.

"Wait here."

"Hey, where you going?"

Running toward him, I called, "Allen!"

He stopped and turned. "Hey, man."

"Hi! I need to tell you something."

"What is it?"

I closed my eyes and took a breath. "Remember that fight you had with Mark Matts, the one when you brought your cousins and Mark brought his friends and stuff?"

"Oh yeah. That's one day I will never

forget," he said with a smile and a chuckle.

"Well, remember, like right after the fight, you went to rest over by the stables next to the strawberry field?"

"Yeah, sure do."

At this point I really began to struggle.

"Well, I…uh…Mark…and…Trev…" I looked straight into the brutal[48] scar[49] just outside his right eye. My scar.

Allen saw me staring at it. He gave me a knowing look. "Hey, man. We were just kids."

I paused momentarily. "You mean you knew it was me the whole time?"

"Yeah," he said nodding, "I knew."

"How?"

"Your green Schwinn Stingray. You were the only kid in the neighborhood who had one."

It took a minute for it all to sink in… For all this time, I had lived with a secret that was never really one.

"Well, I just wanted to say, uh, Allen, I'm really, really, really, sorry I did that."

---

[48] brutal: very mean, cruel, and violent
[49] scar: a permanent mark left on your skin from a cut or wound

"It's okay, man. Really, it's okay."

"But the scar..."

"Hey. I've gotten used to it. And it's a great conversation piece," he added with a smile. I just stood there.

"Listen, we do a lot of stupid things as kids and I accept your apology and all, but there's really no need to feel bad about it. Really." He sounded like he meant it.

"Well, I just really want you to know that I don't know what came over me and I want you to know that I never hated you or anything. I just, I don't know…I just picked up that rock and…"

"Hey, Will. I know hate had nothing to do with it." He looked right in my eyes. "I know how you felt."

I looked at him for a couple of seconds. "Would you like to come meet my wife?"

"I really can't. I have to get going."

"Oh, okay. Uh..."

"Well good luck, man," he said as he held out his hand.

"Good luck," I said. I shook his hand, focusing on the feel of it. Allen turned around and walked away. I turned and looked back towards Anne, who was still standing among our three pieces of luggage. Once more I turned to look for Allen, but he had disappeared into the crowd.

"Who was he?" Anne asked as I walked back toward her.

Again, I looked at the crowd. "An old friend," I replied. "A really good, old childhood friend."

As we made our way out of the airport, we walked without saying a word. All I could do was think about how I had disfigured his face. The scar was brutal. Yet Allen had granted me a pass. He had forgiven me.

Now, I guess it was my turn to forgive myself. Hopefully, this is one scar that will go away.

4114U
(Information For You!)

Written by:
Lynn Dubenko, Ph.D - Child/Family Psychologist
Janet Orr - 3rd Grade Teacher
Stew Montgomery - Religious Scholar
Colleen Ster - Research/Development & Design

Our intent is that you will read through this 4114U section with your parent or guardian. Please read and discuss the tips and tools provided as you process this information together. Our goal is for you to create a game plan to help you to navigate through the stressful situations of peer pressure and identify your true friends.

A parent's job is to give their children the tools needed to navigate, and to be active participants in solving problems that may come their way in life. Peer pressure can be very unsettling for children, and by reviewing the following pages together, you can develop a game plan of action.

- Take the Self-Reflection Test
- Quality Friendship Test
- Who's in Your Bucket? Activity
- Positive Peer Pressure Cycle

Hopefully, this book will open up a wonderful world of communication where you and your child can safely navigate through tough situations together.

Action Steps To Help Families Emotionally

Written by:
Lynn Dubenko, Ph.D-Child/Family Psychologist

Peer Pressure Cycle

```
            Beliefs
     ↗              ↘
Self-Value          Choices
     ↖              ↙
            Actions
```

⇨ Your beliefs guide your choices.
⇨ Your choices guide your actions.
⇨ Your actions impact your self-value/self-worth.

Peer pressure occurs when our peers influence these beliefs, choices, and actions. How can we tell if peer pressure is good or bad? Sometimes peer pressure can make us better friends, athletes, or students. Sometimes though, we compromise our beliefs and make choices that endanger ourselves, hurt others, and damage our self-esteem. Ask yourself these questions to begin identifying negative peer pressure:

- **Belief:** Is the behavior consistent with my belief system?
- **Choice:** Do I feel comfortable, safe, and able to say "no?" Do I have the power to say "No!" or do I give the power to someone else?
- **Action:** Can I ask "why" my friends want me to act this way?
- **Self-Value:** How do I feel about myself both during and after I am with my friends?

It is important for kids to understand that their thoughts and actions determine who they are today, as well as, the adult they are going to become. They are faced with situations every day that challenge this sense of self, consuming their thoughts and turning their mind into a battlefield. Just like a soldier would train for battle or a chess player would make their next move, kids need to develop a clear sense of character and self-confidence to help guide their thoughts during decision-making. The ultimate goal is to equip them with the skills to make the difficult and often unpopular decisions, particularly when presented with the mental and emotional tug-of-war over drug and alcohol use, peer abuse, and intimacy, among others.

"Tug of War"
The Mental Battle

Imagine a time when you may have felt pulled in two different directions. What were the thoughts that went through your head at that time? How did you decide whether to go along with the group or stand up for what you believe in? What were some of the thoughts that went through Will's mind?

Social Exclusion					Social Acceptance
I will be teased.	I won't have anyone to sit with at lunch.	I won't have a partner in class or sports.	I will belong to a group of friends.	I will be invited to all the parties.	I will have social status and power.

Parents: while decision-making is often tricky for adults, it is even more difficult for adolescents. Research has shown that, although their "decision-making center" (frontal lobe) of the brain is not fully developed until young adulthood, their "emotion center" (limbic system) is fully developed by their teenage years. This means that when adolescents are faced with peer pressure their brains will naturally be tugged more towards emotional reasoning. So, how can you help balance this struggle in the emotional direction?

- First, validate the thoughts and feelings they expressed in the activity above. Do not discount their emotional reasoning. It's normal, and often productive, to have those thoughts; they just need to be balanced to help develop stronger reasoning skills.

- Next, initiate discussions about the consequences of our actions. For instance, how would hurting and embarrassing a friend affect them and their family? How would hurting a friend impact your child's self-esteem?

- Third, help your child identify what kind of person they want to become by completing the next five activities. This will help them determine whether their actions are consistent with their character.

Remember, discussions with your children regarding their thoughts, actions, and consequences will be generalized for future decision-making. There may be moments when they are uncomfortable discussing their decision-making processes with you, so start early, and let these discussions guide later decisions.

Action Steps To Help Families Socially

Written by: Janet Orr
3rd Grade Teacher, Del Mar Union Schools

In today's complicated society, being a good decision-maker is crucial to navigating the complex world around us. As parents and educators, it is critical that we find the time and the means to help our children develop good decision-making skills. As children become adolescents, the decisions they are required to make become more complex, and the results of these decisions have greater consequences. Doors of opportunity begin to open and close based on these decisions.

In order to be a good decision-maker, you need to have a strong sense of self and a firm conviction of your beliefs. Knowing who you are and what you believe in, and making choices based on this knowledge, can empower you to make difficult life decisions. Adolescents who develop a strong self-worth tend to rely on themselves and their belief system for decision-making rather than giving the power to others. Good choices lead to positive actions. Making good choices and engaging in positive actions result in an enhanced self-esteem.

Surrounding yourself with positive peer influences is crucial during the tween and teen years because actions that you take during these years will support the roots of self-esteem that lay the groundwork for the choices and behaviors the rest of your life.

Self-Reflection Checklist
Take Your Personal Inventory-What do you Stand For?

- ☐ I am a good friend.
- ☐ I stand up for my beliefs.
- ☐ I am compassionate.
- ☐ I am trustworthy.
- ☐ I am respectful.
- ☐ I am sensitive.
- ☐ I am responsible.
- ☐ I am loyal.
- ☐ I am optimistic and have a positive attitude.
- ☐ I am negative.
- ☐ I am self-assured.
- ☐ I have self-doubt.
- ☐ I respect my body.
- ☐ I am goal-oriented.
- ☐ I have confidence in my decision-making skills.
- ☐ I am concerned with my social status.
- ☐ I am a leader.
- ☐ I am supportive.
- ☐ I am a good listener.
- ☐ I don't judge others before I get to know them.
- ☐ I am self-absorbed.
- ☐ I am thoughtful and selfless.
- ☐ I am easily influenced by my peers.
- ☐ I go along with what is popular.
- ☐ I see the best in others and encourage them.
- ☐ I recognize/accept that people have different gifts/talents.

 **Friendship Checklist**

Directions for Kids & Parents:
Sit down together and talk through your child's group of friends. Then, determine if their group of friends help to build up or tear down your child's self-esteem.

- ❏ My friends are "24 hours a day/7 days a week Friends."
- ❏ My friends are honest, respectful, and loyal to me.
- ❏ My friends support me and my personal goals.
- ❏ My friends stand up for me in difficult situations.
- ❏ My friends are helpful and kind.
- ❏ I feel comfortable being myself when I am around my group of friends.
- ❏ I feel good about myself after being with my friends.
- ❏ I act differently when I am trying to fit in with my group of friends.
- ❏ My friends want to be in a clique and exclude others.

What characteristics do you look for in a friend?

_____
_____
_____

How are you a good friend to others?

_____
_____
_____

Need a New Set of Friends?

There may come a time when you decide that the best outcome for you will be to find a new group of friends. This can be a very difficult step, but you will be safer, happier, and healthier if you surround yourself with people who support and love you just for being you. Don't feel like your situation is permanent or helpless. Once you begin to seek out new activities, you will naturally meet new people who may eventually become friends. You may even meet someone who introduces you to more people and new activities that will widen your new friend group.

Ways to Make New Friends

To have friends, you have to be a friend. Be true to yourself, though. Friends should like you for who you are and not what they want you to be. If you are not in a supportive group of friends, then check out these ideas for fun ways to meet new people:

- Join a club or organization with people that have the same interests as you.

- Plan a party or invite kids to hang out at your house.

- Join a sport's team.

- Volunteer for an organization that you have a passion for and build bonds with individuals that share your same interests and passions.

- Start a conversation when you go to an event. Give someone a compliment or mention an event coming up. Make sure to smile and make eye contact. Don't fold your arms across your chest, yawn, hang out in a corner, or look bored.

Kids Who's in Your Friend Bucket?

Created by: Lynn Dubenko, Ph.D, Janet Orr, and Colleen Ster

Think about your group of friends. On the lines below, list the friends with whom you have experienced peer pressure and/or whom have gotten you to do something that you are not entirely comfortable doing:

"Peer Pressure Friends"

Directions: Now, put your friends into one of the following buckets:

"24/7 Friend" Bucket
- Can share and trust intimate thoughts and feelings
- Loyal, true friends 24 hours a day, 7 days a week
- Have a positive influence on me
- Feel good about myself after spending time together

"Common Interest Friend" Bucket
- Enjoy each other's company, but don't share secrets
- Someone you have met in a sport or activity

"Friend for a Season" Bucket
- Used to be really close friends but have grown apart
- Continue to have a friendly relationship with them

Knowing confidently who your true friends are is a gift. By identifying your friends as "24/7 Friends," "Common Interest Friends, or "Friends for a Season," you are identifying where to invest your time and energy on friendships. Being upset about a friendship that is no longer fruitful is a waste of your time and energy. It is okay to be friends with someone for "Just a Season." Some people come and go in our lives for a purpose or life lesson, and even though it may be hurtful when the friendship fizzles, it is okay to classify them as a "Friend for a Season."

Kids & Parents: Fitting in with Peers

Everyone wants to fit in with their peers. As Paul Harrington points out in *The Secret to Teen Power*, "Whether we like to admit it or not, most of us want love and respect from everyone around us. It's all about that tribal vibe, that feeling of fitting in, of belonging, of being appreciated and loved."

If we recognize the significant, direct influence that our child's peer group has on our child's life, then we need to help our children identify and nurture healthy friendships. Get to know your child's peer group, and recognize the direct impact that these friends can have on your child. Figure out a time to best communicate with your child, reaffirm their self-worth and self-value, and reiterate to them that they have the power to make good choices and decisions.

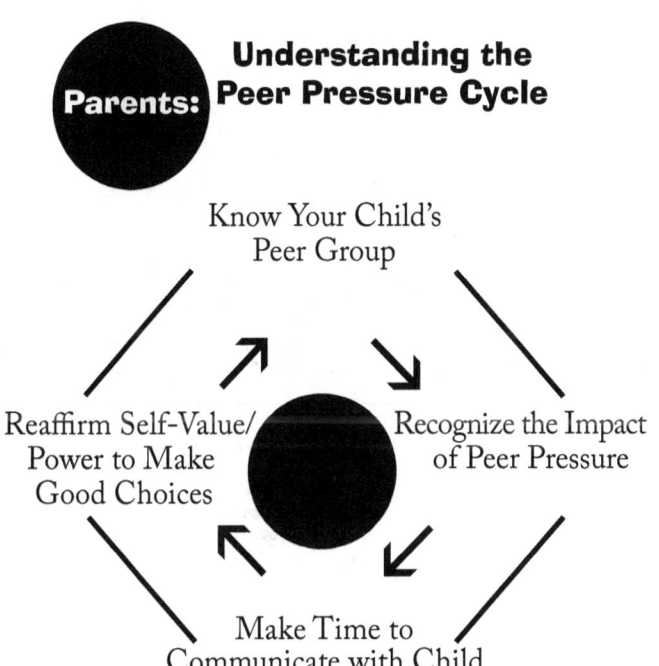

Parents: Understanding the Peer Pressure Cycle

Know Your Child's Peer Group

Reaffirm Self-Value/ Power to Make Good Choices

Recognize the Impact of Peer Pressure

Make Time to Communicate with Child

⇨ Regardless of our age, we all want to have friends. If we can teach our child how to choose those "24/7 Friends," then we have given them a gift for life.

⇨ Read the following "Role Playing Scripts" to help talk through some possible peer pressure situations.

Role Playing Scripts

Created by: Adria O'Donnell, Psy.D • Drawings by Garrett Richie

How to Process Peer Pressure

Witnessing or experiencing peer pressure can be very upsetting. By preparing yourself before a situation occurs, you will have the necessary tips and tools in your back pocket to pull out and utilize. Practice the lines below to give you ideas on how to respond to peer pressure, then use the lines and picture below to write your own script.

- "This is mean. I really don't want to do this."
- "I changed my mind—I don't want to do this."
- "This is making me feel bad. I don't want to say that."
- "This doesn't sound like a good idea. I want out."
- "This isn't cool. I don't want to do this."
- "I can just tell that this is going to go wrong and I'm gonna get busted. Forget it!"

_____
_____
_____

Action Steps To Help Families Spiritually

When a person goes through a difficult time in life, they may often question their belief system or their house of worship. They may wonder why this bad thing is happening to them. According to Dr. Harold Koenig's book, *The Healing Power of Faith*, his research indicates that when people are faced with health problems or life challenges, it is the individuals with strong belief systems who have the best overall, positive recovery. When people can believe in something bigger than themselves, they can often heal faster and experience less pain.

Having a strong connection with others, yourself, and a belief system can help you work through this difficult time and heal. Experiencing peer pressure is extremely painful and you need to know that there is hope. Nobody—adult or child—is strong enough to go through peer pressure alone.

In-depth 4114U: Change of Heart
Written by: Stew Montgomery, MACL

Jason never did anything to us. Jason had never done anything to us. Yet lunchtime after lunchtime, day after day, week after week, we would pester him. We would call him names, we would throw small pebbles at him, and we would laugh at his clothes. I knew that it was hurtful. I knew it was not the sort of thing that I wanted to do; but, at the same time, I was afraid of what my friends would say if I stopped. I was afraid of what my friends would do if I actually tried to be Jason's friend. I wanted to be kind to Jason, yet more than that I wanted to liked and accepted by my friends. Peer pressure is not necessarily a negative thing. Sometimes our friends encourage us to do good things, to be more like the people we want to be. On the other hand, peer pressure can also be used to exploit a very real need in each and every one of us—the need to be loved, to be cared for, and to feel like we belong. Some people would tell us that we do not belong unless we are willing to do the things they tell us to do; sometimes, these are things that we would rather not do. If we are to have the strength to become the sort of person we want to be, our sense of belonging must flow from a deep source. For some people, that is their family; for some people that is their community; for some people that is their belief in God who created them and therefore loves them for who they are. Once we know we fit in somewhere, it gives us the support to be ourselves in every situation. As we begin to develop friendships, we can choose to spend time with friends who help us be who we truly are. As we continue to feel loved, we can begin to invite others to belong. Mother Teresa, someone who spent most of her life working with people who others insisted didn't belong, said, "If we have no peace, it is because we have forgotten that we belong to each other." Through our words, our actions, and our motions, we can help create the sort of group where people feel invited, wanted, and like they belong. If you are interested in helping to create this kind of environment, you may start by praying this prayer:

"God, thank you for the fact that I belong. Help me to remember this when people are pressuring me to do things I don't want to do. Help me to find friends who will help me be the person I am meant to be and help me to be the sort of person who helps other people feel like they belong.

Amen.

About our Experts:

• Lynn M. Dubenko, Ph.D.

Dr. Lynn Dubenko, the founder of Vita Pondera Wellness, www.vitapondera.com, is a licensed clinical psychologist who specializes in health psychology (PSY22882). Dr. Dubenko's clinical experience and training include time at Pitt Memorial Hospital (North Carolina) and Rady Children's Hospital (San Diego), working with cardiac and pulmonary rehabilitation, pediatric hematology & oncology, and stress-related medical conditions. In addition, she has extensive experience working with children diagnosed with chronic pain and their families, treating a variety of conditions, including migraine and tension headaches, abdominal pain, irritable bowel syndrome (IBS), fibromyalgia, chronic regional pain syndrome (CRPS), myofascial (muscular) pain, and injury-related pain.

In her private practice, Dr. Dubenko provides individual and group therapy for all ages, primarily by using cognitive behavioral, mindfulness, and acceptance-based approaches to manage general stress, anxiety, and chronic illness. She also frequently uses biofeedback techniques, relaxation, and guided imagery. Lastly, Dr. Dubenko provides presurgical evaluations for those undergoing transplant, bariatric, or spinal surgeries.

Outside her practice, Dr. Dubenko enjoys mentoring doctoral students and spending time with her husband and two daughters.

• Stew Montgomery, MACL

Solana Beach Presbyterian Church:
Associate Minister of Students & Families

Stew Montgomery works with high school students at Solana Beach Presbyterian Church and has his Masters degree in Christian Leadership from Fuller Seminary. He has been working in youth ministry since 1999, serving in multiple churches and other non-profit settings. Stew loves to help students develop a healthy sense of self that will help them navigate through the increasingly disconnected and high pressure high school environment. Stew lives with his wife Annie and three sons Isaac, Ryder and Asher in Carlsbad, CA.

• Adria O'Donnell, Psy.D
www.drodonnell.com

Dr. Adria O'Donnell is a licensed clinical psychologist practicing in San Diego. Since 2001, she has specialized in working with children and adolescents, with a specialization in teen girls. Her foci are on social skills training for adolescents, learning disabilities, tech-aggression and relational aggression, a more covert form of bullying often used by girls.

In these areas, Dr. O'Donnell has become a coveted public speaker and has developed several pioneering programs. She helped create the "Girls ROCK" program for the Junior League of Pasadena and two programs for grammar ("Brave Talk") and middle and high school aged kids ("Staight Talk"), which teaches conflict resolution skills and assertiveness training.

Dr. Adria speaks locally about the effects of technology on teen's social and emotional development. Her lively workshops bring the timely, latent issues of psychological aggression and victimization in middle school age girls to the fore.

Dr. O'Donnell earned her Bachelor's Degree at the University of San Diego in Communication and Hispanic Studies, attended the University of Granada, Spain, and earned her Doctorate from the California School of Professional Psychology, San Diego.

• Janet Orr
Del Mar Union School District:
Third Grade Teacher

From an early age, Janet knew that, in her professional life, she would be working with children. She received her bachelor degree in Child Development from San Diego State University. After completing her degree, she taught for several years in the San Diego City Schools Children's Center Program. Janet earned her California Teaching Credential from Point Loma Nazarene University. Although she has taught many grades, Janet has spent the last seventeen years teaching third grade in the Del Mar Union School District.

Web Links:

- Bully Safe USA
  http://www.bullysafeusa.com
- Committee for Children
  http://www.cfchildren.org
- Common Sense Media's free Digital Literacy and Citizenship Curriculum
  http://www.commonsensemedia.org/educators
- Connect Safely
  http://www.connectsafely.org
- Family Online Safety Institute
  http://www.fosi.org
- Kidshealth.org
  http://www.kidshealth.org/kid
- SafeKids.com
  http://www.safeteens.com
- Stop Bullying Now! U.S. Department of Health and Human Services
  http://www.stopbullyingnow.hrsa.gov/kids
- TheCoolSpot.gov
  http://www.thecoolspot.gov/pressures/asp.

References for Adults:

- Bronson, PO and Ashley Merryman. *NurtureShock*. New York: Hatchette Book Group, 2009.
- Farber, Adele and Elaine Mazlish. *How to Talk So Kids Will Listen & Listen So Kids Will Talk*. New York: Harper Collins, 1980.
- Fried, SuEllen and Dr. Paula Fried. *Bullies, Targets and Witnesses: Helping Children Break the Pain Chain*. Lanham, MD: Rowman & Littlefield Education, 2009.
- Harrington, Paul. *The Secret to Teen Power*. New York: Simon and Schuster, 2009.
- Heyman, Richard. *How to Say it to Teens: Talking About the Most Important Topics of Their Lives*. New York: Penguin Group (USA) Inc., 2001.
- Koenig, Harold G, M.D. *The Healing Power of Faith: Science Explores Medicines Last Great Frontiers*. New York: Simon & Schuster, 1999.
- Loomans, Diana with Julia Godoy. *What All Children Want Their Parents to Know: 12 Keys to Raising a Happy Child*. Califirnia: Publisher's Group West, 2005.
- Neufeld, Gordon and Gabor Mate. *Hold On To Your Kids: Why Parents Need to Matter More Than Peers*. New York: Ballantine Books, 2006.
- Roizen, Michael F., MD, Mehmet C. Oz, MD and Ellen Rome MD. *You: The Owner's Manuel for Teens: Guide to a Healthy Body and Happy Life*. New York: Simon & Schuster, 2011.

References for Kids (Grade Level):

- Auer, Jim. *Standing Up to Peer Pressure*. Indiana: Abbey Press, 2003. (K-3)
- Boelts, Maribeth. *Those Shoes*. Massachusetts: Candlewick Press, 2009. (K-2)
- Covey, Sean. *The 6 Most Important Decisions You'll Ever Make*. New York: Fireside-A Division of Simon & Schuster, 2009. (7-12)
- Christopher, Matt. *Body Check*. New York: Little, Brown and Company, 2003. (4-7)
- Estes, Eleanor. *The Hundred Dresses*. New York: Houghton Mifflin Harcourt, 2004. (1-6)
- Harrington, Paul. *The Secret to Teen Power*. New York: Simon and Schuster, 2009. (5-12)
- Kaufman, Gershen, Lev Raphael, & Pamela Espeland. *Stick Up for Yourself: Every Kid's Guide to Personal Power & Positive Self-Esteem*. Minnesota: Free Spirit Press, 1999. (5-12)
- Lewis, Barbara. *What Do You Stand For?* Minnesota: Free Spirit Press, 2005. (7-12)
- Lowry, Lois. *The Giver*. New York: Delacorte Press, 1993. (6-9)
- Meyer, Joyce. *Battlefield of the Mind for Kids*. New York: Faith Words, 2006. (K-6)
- Meyer, Joyce. *Battlefield of the Mind for Teens*. New York: Faith Words, 2006. (7-12)
- Otoshi, Kathryn. *One*. San Rafael, CA: Ko Kids Books, 2008. (K-1)
- Paterson, Katherine. *Bridge to Terabithia*. New York: HarperCollins Publisher, 1977. (4-8)
- Raum, Elizabeth. *Peer Pressure*. Chicago, IL: Heinemann Library, 2008. (4-8)
- Richards, Susan. *Joshua T. Bates Takes Charge*. New York: Random House, 1993. (4-8)
- Romain, Trevor. *Cliques, Phonies, & Other Baloney*. Minnesota: Free Spirit Press, 1998. (3-8)
- Spinelli, Jerry. *Fourth Grade Rats*. New York: Scholastic, 1991. (3-6)

In-depth 4114U Concepts:

Page 1: Dread of moving
Page 3: Guilt
Page 8: Taking pride
Page 11: Healthy encouragement
Page 13: Learning social skills/group entry
Page 16: Healthy friendship
Page 23: Teasing a sibling
Page 28: Assessment of friendships
Page 36: Dishonesty
Page 39: Identity, being part of a group
Page 42: Secrecy
Page 43: Standing up for a friend
Page 44: Name-calling, going along with the crowd
Page 45: Revenge
Page 46: Peer pressure, manipulation
Page 48: Making choices: right vs. wrong, self-talk
Page 49: Fear of rejection
Page 52: Anxiety from peer pressure
Page 53: Making good decisions
Page 55: Peer Pressure
Page 57: Fear
Page 59: Anxiety
Page 60: Emotion management
Page 62: Feelings of regret and remorse
Page 63: Self-talk
Page 65: Feelings of remorse
Page 66: Reconciliation
Page 69: Apology
Page 70: Forgiveness
Page 71: Moving forward, overcoming emotions, and forgiving yourself

Book Club Discussion Questions:

1. Have you ever been peer pressured to do something that you didn't want to do?

2. Which of Will's friends remind you of yourself and why?

3. What characteristics do you look for in a friend?

4. How do you think you are a good friend to others?

5. Why does Will have so much trouble forgiving himself for something he did as a kid years ago?

6. Learning to forgive is a powerful gift. Are you able to forgive people who have wronged you?

7. With what personal issue have you had a "mental battle" or "tug of war"?

8. Research shows that most people judge others in 30 seconds. Do you judge people in 30 seconds or do you get to know them before you form an opinion? Is it fair to judge a person in 30 seconds?

9. We all have different gifts and talents. Do you accept people for who they are or do you judge people who are different from you and/or force them to do things you want them to do?

10. List some ways you can meet a new set of friends if your current group of friends are not being supportive and respectful of you?

11. On page 42, the story talks about a secret hiding place. Do you think you should have secrets from your parents?

www.ingramcontent.com/pod-product-compliance
Lightning Source LLC
Chambersburg PA
CBHW071737090426
42738CB00011B/2513